POCKET HOTTIES

HARRY STYLES

INSPIRATIONAL QUOTES AND OBSERVATIONS ON LIFE

ULYSSES PRESS

Independently authored and published. This work is not associated with or authorized by Harry Styles.

Published by:
Uysses Press
PO Box 3440
Berkeley, CA 94703
www.ulyssespress.com

ISBN: 978-1-64604-645-4

Printed in India
10 9 8 7 6 5 4 3 2 1

Acquisitions editor: Claire Sielaff
Managing editor: Claire Chun
Editors: Barbara Schultz, Renee Rutledge
Design and layout: Winnie Liu

STYLE

STYLE

"

I think if you get something
that you feel amazing in, it's
like a superhero outfit. Clothes
are there to have fun with and
experiment with and play with.

"

STYLE

"

You can never be overdressed.
There's no such thing.

"

STYLE

"

Now I'll put on something that
feels really flamboyant, and I
don't feel crazy wearing it.

"

STYLE

"

I'll go in shops sometimes, and I just find myself looking at the women's clothes thinking they're amazing.

"

STYLE

"

There's so much joy to be had
in playing with clothes.

"

STYLE

"

What's feminine and what's
masculine, what men are wearing
and what women are wearing—it's
like there are no lines anymore.

"

STYLE

"

I think the moment you feel
more comfortable with yourself,
it all becomes a lot easier.

"

STYLE

"

I don't think being beautiful or feeling
beautiful is about looking good.

"

Dazed Digital, November 15, 2021

STYLE

“

As a kid I definitely liked fancy dress.

”

RELA TION SHIPS

RELATIONSHIPS

"

A lot of the time, the way it's portrayed is that I only see women in a sexual way. But I grew up with just my mum and sister, so I respect women a lot.

"

RELATIONSHIPS

"

My parents were amazingly
supportive.

"

RELATIONSHIPS

"

I couldn't reach her face.

"

On his first kiss,
Twist magazine, 2012

RELATIONSHIPS

"

I just wanted it to be a normal date.

"

On his Central Park date with Taylor Swift,
Rolling Stone, April 18, 2017

RELATIONSHIPS

"

I find ambition really attractive too—if someone's good at something they love doing. I want someone who is driven.

"

RELATIONSHIPS

"

I've got a really good family, I've
got great friends around me.

"

E! News, November 25, 2013

RELATIONSHIPS

"

I'm quite old-fashioned. I like going out to dinner. You have the chance to talk to somebody and get to know them better.

"

Seventeen magazine, October 10, 2012

RELATIONSHIPS

"

If I was at home and I asked
[my mum] to get me a drink,
she'd be like, 'You know
where the glasses are.'

"

RELATIONSHIPS

"

The one subject that hits the
hardest is love, whether it's
platonic, romantic, loving
it, gaining it, losing it ...

"

RELATIONSHIPS

"

Whenever I've done stuff in
film or music videos, I often put
secret messages in for friends.

"

HIMSELF

"

I never like it when a celebrity goes
on Twitter and says, 'This isn't true!'
It is what it is; I tend not to do that.

"

HIMSELF

"

I meditate and pray before going
onstage—it helps me focus.

"

HIMSELF

"

I knew I really enjoyed performing,
and even at quite a young age
got a real buzz from it.

"

HIMSELF

"

I wanted to succeed when I grew up.

"

HIMSELF

"

I can see how you could get dragged
into the bad stuff, but I've got good
friends around me, good family. I
think I've got my head screwed on.

"

The Sun, October 2012

HIMSELF

"

I definitely consider myself to be
more spiritual than religious.

"

Another Man magazine, Autumn/Winter 2016

HIMSELF

"

I definitely believe in karma.

"

HIMSELF

"

I find writing to be very
therapeutic—I think it's when I allow
myself to be most vulnerable.

"

The New York Times, May 11, 2017

HIMSELF

"

In the early years, I spent a lot of
time worrying about what would
happen and getting things wrong
and [...] doing the wrong thing.

"

All Things Considered, NPR, February 27, 2020

LIFE

"

I think with the therapy thing, I
just realized I was just getting in
my own way [...] I've definitely felt
it have an impact on my life.

"

LIFE

"

We have a choice[:] To
Live or To Exist. :)

"

LIFE

"

Eating toast in the shower is
the ultimate multitask.

"

LIFE

"

Be a lover. Choose love. Give love.

"

In response to the 2017 Manchester bombing,
In concert, Mexico, May 23, 2017

LIFE

Work hard. Play hard. Be kind.

Twitter, December 22, 2011

LIFE

"

Be nice to nice.

"

LIFE

"

I've always made myself take
a step back, to kind of just
see it as what it is, so that it
doesn't become normal life.

"

On being in the public eye,
Who We Are: One Direction: Our Autobiography

LIFE

"

Meditation has helped with
worrying about the future
less, and the past less.

"

LIFE

"

Everyone should just be
who they want to be.

"

LIFE

"

I went in for the first time
and I cried, because I just felt
like I *had* somewhere.

"

On his home in North London,
Vogue, December 2020

LIFE

"

I feel like my relationship with
L.A. has changed a lot. I've kind
of accepted that I don't have to
live here anymore; for a while
I felt like I was supposed to.

"

LIFE

"

Between the two [fans and
friends] I'm incredibly lucky to
have an environment where I
feel comfortable being myself.

"

SUCCESS

"

You're never going to get used to
walking into a room and have
people screaming at you.

"

SUCCESS

"

There's a lot of things that come with
the life you could get lost in. But you
have to let it be what it is. I've learned
not to take everything too seriously.

"

SUCCESS

"

I don't think you can ever get used to being this famous. I've learnt how to keep things separate or at a distance.

"

SUCCESS

"

You kind of want someone who
knows what they're talking about
to tell you if you're any good or
not instead of just your mum.

"

About *The X Factor*,
NPR, December 9, 2012

SUCCESS

"

You get moments all the time
that kind of make you pinch
yourself, some of them make
you quite emotional.

"

Mirror, November 19, 2012

SUCCESS

"

Winning a BRIT was a big moment
because we were just so excited to
be at the awards in the first place.
Selling out Madison Square Garden
was pretty amazing, too. Then
we woke to the news that our UK
tour was sold out. It was crazy.

"

SUCCESS

"

I love the band, and would never rule
out anything in the future. The band
changed my life, gave me everything.

"

Another Man magazine, June 7, 2017

SUCCESS

"

I think if you're making what you
want to make, then ultimately
no one can tell you you're
unsuccessful, because you're
doing what makes you happy.

"

NPR, February 27, 2020

SUCCESS

"

If you just think that's how life
is, that's when you lose touch.
It's good to have people who
can tell you you're an idiot and
tell you when you're wrong.

"

Another Man magazine, June 7, 2017

SUCCESS

"

The kindest thing [the
fans] have done for me is
probably given me a job.

"

Capital FM, YouTube, December 12, 2019

SUCCESS

"

I like to challenge myself and
do something different, and
movies are definitely where I feel
most out of my comfort zone.

"

Dazed Digital, November 15, 2021

SUCCESS

"

Bringing people together is
the thing I'm most proud of.

"

SUCCESS

"

It hasn't become normal to me
at all. I hope it never will.

"

On the massive scale of One
Direction's tour production,
Who We Are: One Direction: Our Autobiography

SUCCESS

"

We got the worst room in the house!

"

On *The X Factor* lodgings,
One Direction Video Diaries for *The X Factor*,
Week 1, Fatima Payne on YouTube

SUCCESS

"

We wouldn't be here
without you guys.

"

On the support of the fans,
One Direction Video Diaries for *The X Factor*,
Week 3, Fatima Payne on YouTube

SOCIETY AND CULTURE

SOCIETY AND CULTURE

"

Most of the stuff that hurts
me about what's going on at
the moment is not politics, it's
fundamentals. Equal rights.

"

SOCIETY AND CULTURE

"

You can tell far too much
about a person by which
Monopoly piece they play as.

"

SOCIETY AND CULTURE

"

I was promised when I got
into this job there would be
NO! MORE! MATHS!

"

In concert, New York, September 1, 2022

SOCIETY AND CULTURE

"

Anytime you're putting barriers
up in your own life, you're
just limiting yourself.

"

SOCIETY AND CULTURE

"

I do like food! I eat it every day.

"

Capital FM, YouTube, December 12, 2019

SOCIETY AND CULTURE

"

A room full of people just loving
each other is so powerful.

"

Dazed Digital, November 15, 2021

SOCIETY AND CULTURE

"

I just think she's amazing—she's
definitely one of the most exciting
artists working right now for sure.

"

On Lizzo,
BBC Radio 1 Live Lounge, December 2019

SOCIETY AND CULTURE

"

Who didn't grow up wanting to
be a superhero, you know?

"

Dazed Digital, November 15, 2021

SOCIETY AND CULTURE

"

Any time you are looking at the
world through someone else's lens
and exploring different emotions, it
feels like a benefit in so many ways.

"

Dazed Digital, November 15, 2021

MUSIC

"

With the people I grew up listening to, like Elvis, David Bowie, The Stones, and people like that, it's part of the show because it's fun, and I just like to have fun with it.

"

Audacy Music, YouTube, December 6, 2019

MUSIC

"

'Dreams' was the first song I
knew all the words to. I used to
sing it in the car with my mom.

"

On listening to Fleetwood Mac as a child,
NPR, February 27, 2020

MUSIC

"

That's the amazing thing about
music: there's a song for every
emotion. Can you imagine a world
with no music? It would suck.

"

E! News, November 25, 2013

MUSIC

"

I heard some stuff recently from
Julian Casablancas, and his solo
stuff is amazing. If I could write
with anyone, it would be him.

"

MUSIC

"

You're always going to write and
draw inspiration from things that
you're feeling, things that you've felt.

"

E! News, November 25, 2013

MUSIC

"

I think when you're writing songs, it's
impossible to not draw on personal
experiences, whether it be traveling,
or girls, or anything. Just emotions.

"

E! News, November 25, 2013

MUSIC

"

You get a lot of who you are
as a musician across through
the music you write. If you're
writing your own music, then it's
important to be really honest.

"

MUSIC

"

Who's to say that young girls who
like pop music—short for popular,
right?—have worse musical taste
than a 30-year-old hipster guy?
That's not up to you to say.

"

MUSIC

"

Music is something that's
always changing.

"

Rolling Stone, April 18, 2017

MUSIC

"

The people that I looked up to in music—Prince and David Bowie and Elvis and Freddie Mercury and Elton John—they're such showmen.

"

MUSIC

"

I didn't want to make the same
music we were making in the band.
Not because I didn't like it, I just
wanted it to be a different thing.

"

MUSIC

"

This is a family show! Or is it?

"

MUSIC

"
Shania Twain is so good.
"

MUSIC

"

Always feel lucky when *Grease*
songs come on the radio.

"

MUSIC

"

['Fine Line'] is one of my favorite
songs on the album.

"

MUSIC

"

I think [Rosalia's] voice is amazing. I
think she is one of the most talented
people working in the world today.

"

Capital FM, YouTube, December 12, 2019

MUSIC

"
What's with all the fruit references?
I don't know. They seem to be
happening by accident.
"

Capital FM, YouTube, December 12, 2019

MUSIC

"

There are twelve Easter eggs on *Fine
Line* and see if you can find them.

"

"

The hardest song to finish [on *Fine Line*] was 'Watermelon Sugar.' We wrote it in a day and then it took about a year to finish, which was very frustrating.

"

Capital FM, YouTube, December 12, 2019

MUSIC

"

The fun thing is, you can write a
love song that's not always in the
traditional sense—it doesn't always
have to be romantic or even about
a person at all, if you don't want.

"

"

When I wrote ['Treat People
with Kindness'] I wasn't sure if I
really liked it or really hated it.

"

MUSIC

"

[*Fine Line*] was so much more
joyous than the last [album], so
the music and everything around
it feels a lot more joyous.

"

MUSIC

"

I'm quite handy with a kazoo.

"

One Direction Video Diaries for *The X Factor*,
Week 3, Fatima Payne on YouTube